THE GHOSTLY TALES OF MADISON

Published by Arcadia Children's Books
A Division of Arcadia Publishing
Charleston, SC
www.arcadiapublishing.com

Copyright © 2024 by Arcadia Children's Books
All rights reserved

Spooky America is a trademark of Arcadia Publishing, Inc.

First published 2024
Manufactured in the United States

Designed by Jessica Nevins
Images used courtesy of Shutterstock.com; p. 38 EQRoyShutterstock.com.

ISBN: 978-1-4671-9774-8
Library of Congress Control Number: 2024939040

Notice: The information in this book is true and complete to the best of our knowledge. It is offered without guarantee on the part of the author or Arcadia Publishing. The author and Arcadia Publishing disclaim all liability in connection with the use of this book.

All rights reserved. No part of this book may be reproduced or transmitted in any form whatsoever without prior written permission from the publisher except in the case of brief quotations embodied in critical articles and reviews.

Spooky America

THE GHOSTLY TALES OF MADISON

ANNA LARDINOIS

Adapted from Madison Ghosts and Legends by Anna Lardinois

Wisconsin

Madison

Table of Contents & Map Key

Welcome to Spooky Madison!. 3

Chapter 1. A Very Spooky School. 7
- **1** Camp Randall Stadium
- **2** Bascom Hall
- **3** Science Hall
- **4** Arboretum

5 Chapter 2. A Creepy Capitol Building 29

Chapter 3. On With the Show! 39
- **6** Magestic Theater
- **7** Barrymore Theater
- **8** The Orpheum Theater

9 Chapter 4. A Most Haunted Cemetery. 51

10 Chapter 5. The Ghost of Seminole Highway 59

Chapter 6. Mysterious Waterways. 67
- **11** Lake Mendota
- **12** Lake Monona
- **13** Lake Waubesa
- **14** Lake Kegonsa
- **15** Lake Wingra

16 Chapter 7. The Beast of Bray Road. 93

A Ghostly Goodbye 103

Welcome to Spooky Madison!

Welcome to Madison, the capital of Wisconsin, home of Bucky Badger, and one of the most haunted cities in the Midwest!

Get ready to read all about the restless spirits that linger in the Capitol building, some very creepy spots on the University of Wisconsin campus, and the ghosts that dwell in the city's most haunted theaters. And that's just for starters!

Not only does Madison have ghosts, it also has some strange creatures lurking on land and slithering through the waterways. Some places claim to be home to a Yeti, a Sasquatch, or even a Chupacabra—a mythical beast said to attack and drink the blood of goats and cattle. Well, Madison can top that! After all, the city has its *own* strange beasts. Yes—beasts with an *s*! There is more than one mysterious creature that calls the Madison area its home! Is there a werewolf in Walworth County? Does a sea serpent slither through the Yahara River chain of lakes? Read the stories and decide for yourself.

Just one more thing—people in Madison use the word *isthmus* a lot. It even appears in this book a few times. If you are not from the area, you might not have heard of an isthmus before. An isthmus is a narrow strip of land that connects two larger landmasses and separates two bodies of water.

Confused? Don't be. If you take a look at a map of Madison, you'll see that downtown Madison sits on an isthmus—the strip of land between Lake Mendota and Lake Monona.

Are you ready to discover why Madison is one of the most haunted cities in the Midwest? Turn the page and start reading. That is, if you dare!

Bascom Hall and statue of Abraham Lincoln

CHAPTER 1

A Very Spooky School

The University of Wisconsin–Madison is the home of Bucky Badger. The school was founded in 1848, the same year Wisconsin became a state. That's over 175 years ago! There is a lot of history on this campus—and a lot of ghosts! Keep reading and you'll see what I mean. In the end, I think you'll agree that this campus certainly has lots of "school spirit."

Camp Randall

Let's start by taking a look at Bucky's haunted home, Camp Randall Stadium. The stadium can hold 80,321 red-and-white-clad Bucky fans. If the only thing you know about the football stadium is how Badger fans go crazy when "Jump Around" is played, you might be surprised to learn that the stadium is considered one of the most haunted sports venues in the country.

However, years before the stadium hosted its first football game in 1917, the land was the site of misery and bloodshed.

The land on which the football stadium stands was once a training ground for an estimated 70,000 Union Army soldiers during the Civil War. The camp was named for Alexander W. Randall, the state's first wartime governor. Later, the camp was also used as a place to imprison Confederate soldiers. Over 1,000 prisoners were held there.

Conditions in Civil War prisoner camps were terrible, and Camp Randall was no exception. There was not enough space or food to support so many prisoners. The camp was overcrowded and dirty. Illnesses like measles, mumps, and pneumonia ran rampant through the camp.

In a letter to his family, Private Paddock of the Nineteenth Wisconsin Regiment wrote about the terrible conditions in the camp. "They die off like rotten sheep. There was eleven die off yesterday and today, and there ain't a day but what there is from two to nine dies," his letter said.

The prison was eventually closed, and the surviving prisoners were transferred to Camp Douglas in Chicago. Camp Douglas had more space and resources to take care of the prisoners. It was a welcome relief for the captured Confederate soldiers.

But sadly, the transfer came too late for the 140 Confederate soldiers who died at Camp Randall. Those unfortunate prisoners of war are now spending the hereafter buried at the nearby Forest Hill Cemetery. They are buried in a mass grave known as Confederate Rest, the northernmost confederate cemetery in the United States.

Many believe the spirits of those Confederate soldiers continue to dwell on the land where they took their last breaths. Football fans have reported seeing the apparitions of Confederate soldiers, still wearing their tattered uniforms, near the stadium—and even inside the Field House!

The next time you attend a University of Wisconsin Badgers football game, you might want to stick close to the people you came with. You certainly don't want to be alone if you run into the eerie spirit of a captive Confederate soldier still trying to make his way home. The undead soldiers may be closer than you think!

Bascom Hall

Camp Randall stadium is hardly the only place to have a ghostly encounter on campus. Another place where you could have a spine-tingling supernatural experience is Bascom Hall. Not only is it one of the best-known buildings on campus—it's also the location of a former graveyard!

The Indigenous peoples who first lived in the area used the land as a burial ground. When white settlers arrived, they also buried their dead there. They used the land as a cemetery from 1837 until 1846. Eventually, it was decided the site would be the home of the new university. Madisonians dug up the graves and moved the bodies to other cemeteries. Well, at least *most* of the bodies. As it turned out, not all the dead made it to a new resting place.

It wasn't until 1918 that people discovered there were still bodies buried on Bascom Hill. It happened when construction workers were preparing the area for the big bronze statue of President Lincoln. The workers were digging a base for the massive statue when they uncovered something unexpected—four human leg bones!

At first, people thought the bones might be those of recent murder victims who had been buried on campus. But, when they took a closer look, they changed their minds. Next to the bones, they found old-fashioned iron nails. They also found a shirt button so old it must have belonged to an early settler. That is when the men realized the leg bones probably belonged to bodies left behind when the graves on the property were moved to build Bascom Hall.

But that is not the end of the story. More bones were found on the site. In 1922, construction workers unearthed the bodies that had once been connected to the leg bones found in 1918. The skeletons were found intact—except for their missing legs, of course!

After doing some research, detectives determined that the bones belonged to William Nelson and Samuel Warren. William died of typhoid in 1837, and Samuel died in 1838 after being struck by lightning.

Because the bones had spent so many decades on the property, everyone involved decided they should stay there. Yes, you are

reading that correctly. To this day, the graves of the two men are still on Bascom Hill. If you've ever taken a photo of the statue of Lincoln, they could be in your picture without you even realizing it!

On the southwest side of the statue, you can find two small brass plates. The plates mark the graves of the men discovered over a hundred years ago. One is marked "W.N. 1837" and the other "S.W. 1838."

What do you think? Are the spirits of William and Samuel the source of the reported paranormal activity in and around Bascom Hall? Or, could it be the restless spirits of those whose bodies were moved from their original resting place? Unless there are even *more* people buried on Bascom Hill still to be discovered? No one knows for sure, but one thing seems certain—Bascom Hill is *very* haunted!

Generations of university students have described hearing strange whispers while walking through the empty rooms inside Bascom Hall. People who have heard the sounds can't quite make out the otherworldly murmurings. Students have searched high and low, but they have not been able to find the source of these spooky sounds. After so many years of ghostly reports, many Madisonians have concluded that some unseen force is trying to communicate with the living.

After all, it's not *just* sounds that have scared visitors at Bascom Hall. Spooky specters can be seen lingering on the hill. Many people have reported seeing a ghostly form walking on the front stairs of Bascom Hall. Some visitors have even claimed to see full-body apparitions near the site of Nelson and Warren's graves.

If you have taken a photo of the Lincoln statue, you may want to take a second look at the image. There are countless reports of visitors capturing orbs and other signs of paranormal activity in photos taken on the hill. Scan the picture carefully. Do you see any unexplained balls of light? If so, you may have captured an orb. Some people believe orbs are otherworldly spirits. If you spot one in your photo, you just might have seen a ghost!

Whatever you believe,  if you visit Bascom Hall, be sure to keep your ears open and your camera ready!

Science Hall

Bascom Hall is not the only building on campus with ghosts. One of the spookiest buildings on campus is just a five-minute walk away: Science Hall, the eerie-looking five-story red brick tower that looms over Park Street. If you believe the stories, this building is even more haunted than it looks!

Maybe all the rumors started because the building has housed the bodies of countless dead people over the years. Of course, it did—it is home to the Department of Anatomy. This is where medical school students learn about the human body by studying and dissecting cadavers, which are dead human bodies. Working with cadavers might be necessary, but it doesn't make them any less creepy.

Until 1956, all the cadavers that medical students used for their studies were housed in this eerie building, and Room 15 served as the morgue, where bodies were stored. Before the building had elevators, cadavers were hoisted to the fourth-floor labs using ropes and pulleys and then passed through the windows. Can you imagine catching a glimpse of that on your way to class?

Unfortunately, there are stories of a few medical students disrespecting the cadavers in the building. There are tales of students pranking each other by tossing amputated fingers out the windows to hit unsuspecting people walking by Science Hall and others of students driving around town with cadavers in their cars.

To make matters even creepier, random body parts have been found in unexpected places throughout Science Hall. In 1974, students were cleaning the storage space in Room 470 when they discovered something startling. A student grabbed a rubber rainboot from the floor. Before tossing it in the trash, the student decided to take a closer look at the boot. That's a good thing, because inside the boot was a preserved human foot with five inches of bone sticking out of it! No one knew how long the foot had been there or who it had belonged to. Later, the mystery foot was sent to the medical school for safekeeping.

Around the same time, a pair of human leg bones was found in the dusty attic. This time, the bones weren't sent to the medical school. No one quite knows how it happened, but a few years later, the same bones turned up in another unexpected place. This time, they were found in a dark corner of Room 443 when it was being cleaned out for renovation.

With all those pranks and misplaced bones, it's no wonder the building is haunted by the restless spirits of people who dedicated their bodies to science. These spirits are not shy about making themselves known to the living in Science Hall. Reports of disembodied footsteps echoing through empty halls are not uncommon. Many people claim to feel an unseen presence when they are in the building. Are these stories a result of overactive imaginations? Or is there really something supernatural happening in the building?

Could the rumored ghosts be the spirits of the cadavers once stored in Room 15? Maybe. It could be worth a visit to the ominous red brick building to decide for yourself.

Arboretum

University ghosts don't just limit themselves to the main campus. UW–Madison ghosts are everywhere, including the Arboretum out on Seminole Highway. Arboretum sounds like a fancy word, but its meaning is pretty easy to understand. An Arboretum is a place where trees and woody plants are grown for scientific and educational purposes.

People have been telling the story of UW–Madison's haunted arboretum since your great-grandmother was a girl. The idea of an arboretum at the university was first proposed in 1911. In 1932, the university acquired 246 acres, and today, the arboretum covers 1,200 acres filled with a variety of trees and plants. But before the arboretum existed, the area was known as Bartlett's Wood and was home to families who farmed in the woods.

One of the people who lived in the woods was Albert Lamson. One summer night, a strange noise awakened Albert from a deep sleep. He yawned and rubbed his eyes, wondering what he had heard. Then, he heard the sound again. This time, he recognized it as the crack of an axe blade biting into a tree. He was puzzled and asked himself why someone would be chopping down a tree in the middle of the night.

For a time, Albert listened to the rhythmic whack of the axe hacking into a tree trunk. Still in bed, he decided not to go investigate, and he soon drifted back to sleep.

The next morning, Albert figured he should find out who had been chopping wood by moonlight in Bartlett's Woods. As soon as he was dressed, Albert headed out into the forest to locate the stumps of the trees he'd heard cut down the night before.

He searched high and low for the tree stumps but could not find them. In fact, he could not find a single tree with as much as a nick in its bark, much less a fresh tree stump. Albert was baffled.

As he was walking back to his house, he encountered a few of his neighbors walking along the same path. The neighbors were also investigating the sounds of the late-night wood chopping. Just like Albert, they hadn't been able to find any evidence that anyone had been in the woods the night before. But each of them was certain they heard the distinct *crack* of a blade against the trunk of a tree.

That night was just the beginning. Throughout the summer and well into the fall, people living in Bartlett's Wood were awoken in the night by the sound of chopping.

The people living in the woods wanted answers. Who was chopping wood at night? Why were they chopping wood under the cover of darkness? Did this person pose any kind of danger? And most importantly, why was there no evidence of chopped trees in the daylight? A

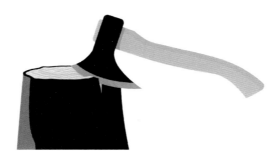

group of area men joined forces to investigate the moonlight axe swinger, but they found no answers.

Before long, people started to suspect something supernatural was happening. How could there be so much wood chopping without any tree stumps or pieces of splintered wood? Maybe, the neighbors thought, this mysterious nighttime wood chopper was actually an otherworldly entity.

The neighbors decided to start patrolling the woods at night when the wood chopper would be in the forest. Only, as the legend goes, most of the men fled the woods in fear before the sounds of wood chopping even began! It seems no one wanted to encounter an unknown axe-wielding being—and who could blame them?

When the fall air turned frosty and snow fell in the woods, the moonlight axe chopping ended just as abruptly as it began. No one ever learned the source of the spine-tingling sounds that briefly haunted Bartlett's Woods. To this day, the mystery still lingers in the memories of the families who lived through these curious events . . . and the eerie question remains:

Does the ghostly wood chopper still haunt the woods?

The only way to find out is to visit the Arboretum for yourself. The grounds are open until ten o'clock each night if you are in the mood for some ghost hunting. But if you go, consider wearing your running shoes, *just in case*.

Wisconsin Capitol Building

A Creepy Capitol Building

Madison was an important city even before Wisconsin became a state. In 1836, when Wisconsin was still just a territory, Madison was chosen as the capital. Over the years, there were a number of different capitol buildings, each with its own strange story.

In 1837, the first capitol building was erected in Madison. Just five years later, blood would stain the floor of the historic building. It was the first time blood was shed in a Wisconsin capitol... and it would not be the last.

During a session on February 11, 1842, James Russell Vineyard, a Democratic politician representing Grant County (a county in southwestern Wisconsin that borders Iowa and Illinois), was arguing with fellow politician Charles C.P. Arndt. He was a Whig who represented most of the eastern part of the state. The Whig Party was a conservative political party in the United States during the 1800s. Alongside the Democratic Party, it was one of the two major parties in the country between the 1830s and the 1850s.

Both men's tempers were still flaring when the session ended.

Instead of leaving after the meeting, Arndt rose from his desk and stormed over to

Vineyard. The pair exchanged bitter words. Eyewitnesses saw Arndt hit Vineyard in the face.

Suddenly, Vineyard drew his gun. Before anyone could stop him, Vineyard shot Arndt. The room full of politicians watched in stunned silence as Arndt spun around from the impact of the shot. He stumbled about while clutching the left side of his chest. Blood gushed from the bullet wound. Minutes later, Arndt was dead.

Authorities arrested Vineyard immediately. The headline-making murder shocked the nation. Vineyard was later returned to his home district to be tried for the killing in the capitol. Unbelievably, Vineyard was acquitted (or freed) on the grounds of self-defense. He even went on to serve as a state assemblymember in 1849.

But many believe the tale of that fateful day does not end there.

The capitol building where Arndt took his last breath no longer stands, but legend has it that the murdered man still roams the land where he lost his life.

Since Arndt's death, two different buildings have been erected there. Both buildings served as Wisconsin state capitols. But, it seems that the destruction of the first capitol building on that property did not release the angry spirit of Charles Arndt. The politician's body is buried in Green Bay, yet many believe his spirit still remains in Madison. Those sensitive to paranormal activity claim to have felt the ghostly presence of Arndt as unexpected cold spots throughout the current building.

Sadly, Arndt's murder was not the last violent death to occur in the capitol and leave a ghostly legacy.

The second capitol building on that spot was built between 1857 and 1869, and it expanded in 1883. It was during that expansion that tragedy struck. On the afternoon of November 8, a tremendous crash echoed throughout Madison. A rolling rumble that followed the crash lasted for more than thirty seconds. The powerful sound could be heard more than two miles away.

When the crashing subsided, it was replaced by screams of terror and moans of pain. It took a few moments for confused Madisonians to understand what had happened. Shockingly, the south wing of the capitol building, where construction workers were on the job, had collapsed! Pleas for help filled the air as airborne debris began to settle over the city.

The cries for help were coming from the construction workers buried beneath tons of rubble. While the men were working, the pillars supporting the construction had given out, causing the south wall of the capitol to fall. Moments later, the roof caved in. Then the problem got even worse. Suddenly, all three stories of the south wing collapsed, trapping an unknown number of workmen in the rubble.

Townspeople rushed to the building to help free the trapped men. When the rescuers arrived, they were horrified to see about

a dozen workmen "hanging by their legs from some of the upper rafters, which were attached to the side walls and did not fall. They became entrapped in this painful position, though flying debris had killed two or three and relieved them from their torture." Other men were buried under more than ten feet of crushed stone and splintered wood.

The rescue took hours, but all the bodies were recovered from the site. In the end, six men died in the ruins of the south wing. Nineteen men were seriously injured in the collapse.

But just because the bodies were taken from the location does not mean the spirits of the dead left the scene of the accident. In fact, some locals believe the south wing of the capitol is now the most haunted area of the building.

There are countless reports of doors opening and slamming shut by themselves. Over the years, employees have claimed to hear the heavy tread of work boots plodding down empty hallways. The sound of the ghostly footfalls echoes in the stillness, sending shivers down the spines of all who hear it.

The second capitol building, where this horrible accident occurred, burned to the ground in 1904. The blaze started when the flame from a gaslight ignited a newly varnished

ceiling. The fire raged for seventeen hours, and when the flames finally died, little was left of the once-grand building. No lives were lost in the fire, but the flames did not rid the land of the spirits that continue to dwell there.

The capitol building that stands in this location today is Madison's third. Visitors are welcome to tour the beautiful, grand building. If you go, you'll learn a great deal of Wisconsin history. And, if you are lucky—or very *unlucky*, depending on your desire for a paranormal experience—you just might experience a few spooky things that don't appear on the tour maps.

Orpheum Theater

On With the Show!

There are haunted theaters across the country, and Madison is no exception. Let's visit a few of the city's most haunted venues.

The Majestic Theater

The Majestic Theater is one of Madison's oldest theaters. It was built in 1906 and has hosted everything from vaudeville shows (a type of entertainment popular in the early 1900s) to modern music performances.

It seems that the ghosts that linger in this historic theater spend most of their time in the balcony. Many theater employees have reported seeing a man sitting in the balcony long after the theater has closed for the evening. What the employees don't realize, at least at first, is that they are looking at an apparition. The supposed man in the balcony? He's a ghost!

Each time the man is spotted, the same thing happens. The employee walks up the stairs to the balcony to escort the man out of the closed theater. But oddly, when the employee finally

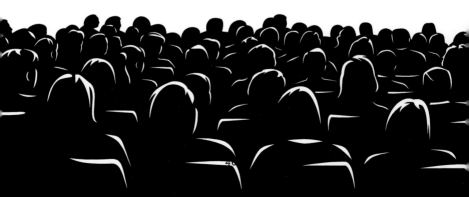

reaches the balcony, there is no trace of the man—almost as if he's disappeared into thin air! There is only one way into and out of the balcony, so there is no way he could have left without walking past the employee. And that is when it dawns on the employee that there is only one possible explanation: The man isn't a man at all. At least, not a *mortal* one!

These strange encounters with the mystery man in the balcony leave employees feeling frightened. So frightened that a few who have encountered the man refuse to work alone in the theater.

But while the ghostly man in the balcony may scare employees, it seems this

otherworldly presence may have a soft spot for artists. Performers have described hearing a disembodied voice encouraging them before their upcoming show.

No one knows who the man in the balcony was in life, but it seems he is content to spend his afterlife in the old theater on King Street.

Barrymore Theatre

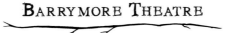

Originally known as the Eastwood Theatre, the Barrymore Theatre opened its doors in 1929. The theater has some unique features, like "twinkling star lights" set into the ceiling. Luckily, those special lights still sparkle for theater-goers to this day.

Like most old theaters today, the Barrymore hosts live music, comedy shows, and films. But *unlike* most old theaters, the Barrymore itself was once the star of the show!

In 2017, the Barrymore was featured in

the documentary *Haunted State: Theatre of Shadows*. The film captures a paranormal investigation into the reportedly haunted building and tells the stories of those who have had supernatural experiences in the theater.

The investigators in the film recorded a shocking range of paranormal activity in the theater. Shortly after they began the investigation, a house light in the theater turned itself on. Then, minutes later, a heavy metal fire door slammed itself shut. And that was just the beginning of strange things inside the Barrymore.

The investigators captured the appearance of orbs on film. Many people who believe in ghosts think orbs are the spirits of the dead moving in the earthly realm. Orbs are glowing balls of light that move through the air on their own.

Orbs can appear in just about any size or color. Sometimes, orbs cannot be seen with the naked eye, but they will appear in photos and video.

The investigators also recorded evidence of electronic voice phenomenon (EVP). Electronic voice phenomena are recorded sounds thought to be the voices of spirits attempting to communicate with the living. These voices cannot be heard without the aid of electronic equipment. The voice in the film was recorded using a device placed in the balcony of the theater. The unseen entity can be heard having a rather unsettling exchange with one of the investigators while the team was recording.

Not all the paranormal encounters at the Barrymore occur inside the theater itself. Many who have been in the basement claim to have seen the apparition of a man. The spirit is dressed in an old-fashioned usher's uniform. The ghostly theater employee is usually spotted with his arm resting on the banister of the basement staircase. The film shows the investigators in the basement, sitting around a table in the dark, hoping to communicate with this apparition.

The investigators placed a flashlight in the center of the table. Flashlights are popular tools for paranormal investigators because they appear to be easy for spirits to turn on and off. Then, they began asking the spirit questions. Remarkably, the camera crew captured the flashlight turning on and off several times without anyone touching it. The investigators believed the spirit was responding to their questions.

If you believe the film, the ghosts are very active at the Barrymore Theatre. If you ever wanted to have your own

ghostly encounter, you might want to see a show at the Barrymore. But be careful—you just might get your wish!

Orpheum Theater

Some say the Orpheum Theater is one of Madison's most haunted buildings. The Art Deco movie palace was completed in 1927. Generations of Madisonians have filled the theater's seats to see films, live performances, and other special events. You might be one of them. But some people come to the theater just to have a supernatural encounter with one of the building's legendary ghosts.

One of the ghosts that haunts the Orpheum is thought to be an usher who reportedly died after falling from the theater's upper balcony. The ghost of the young man has been witnessed seated in the theater house, always alone. But look quickly! Once he is spotted, he often disappears without a trace.

Another well-known spirit in the theater is the specter known as Projectionist Pete. Rumor has it this restless spirit was a former projectionist (a person who operates a film projector) who died in the theater. The ghost is said to be a mischievous one. He often moves objects in the projectionist's booth.

The theater also has a night manager from long ago who is still reporting for shifts

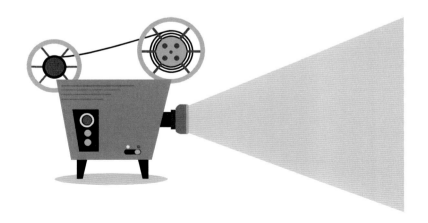

from beyond the grave. The hardworking apparition's disembodied footsteps can be heard throughout the building. As he makes his rounds at closing time, the jingle of unseen keys from his otherworldly key ring echo in the Orpheum's empty halls. Sometimes, he is seen with a shadowy figure who has been spotted cleaning the theater.

Not surprisingly, when the theater is closed, the paranormal activity inside the Orpheum is easier to detect. Muffled conversations can be heard in the empty theater. Some have even reported seeing the apparition of a woman dressed in a lovely gown from a bygone era near the bar. When eyewitnesses move closer to the woman to get a better look, she does what so many Orpheum ghosts do: vanishes without a trace!

Today, when you see a show at the beloved

landmark, just remember you are also visiting the home of some of the city's best-known specters. So stay alert—the person sitting next to you might just be a ghost!

A Most Haunted Cemetery

Historic Forest Hill Cemetery on Speedway Road is just north of Lake Wingra. The 140-acre cemetery was established in 1857, and plenty of famous people are buried there. It is the final resting place of eight Wisconsin governors and some of Madison's most influential historical figures. Legend has it that Forest Hill Cemetery is *also* Madison's most haunted cemetery. Curious ghost hunters have been drawn to the spot for as long as anyone can remember. If you are feeling brave, read on to learn about the spirits that still linger on Speedway Road. If graveyards give you the willies, just skip this chapter.

While most people agree that Forest Hill Cemetery is haunted, they don't agree on *why*. One theory is that the spirits spending their afterlife in the cemetery feel unsettled because their graves are not properly marked.

The cemetery is estimated to contain as many as 339 unmarked graves and unreadable gravestones. Some believe that the spirits

of those buried without a marker or with an unreadable marker are not able to rest peacefully. Could these souls find peace if their names were known to all who passed by their graves? Perhaps...

Another theory is that some spirits lingering here feel unsettled because Forest Hill Cemetery is not their first "final" resting place—but their second or third! Some bodies buried in the cemetery were moved from their original burial site—like those initially buried on Bascom Hill. The belief is that when these bodies were dug up and reburied at Forest Hill,

the spirits connected to the unearthed corpses were no longer at peace.

And can you really blame them? Not only were some of the dead misplaced or even lost during this process, but other bodies once laid to rest beside loved ones were reburied in Forest Hill Cemetery, far away from their family plots. Perhaps these spirits roam in search of those they once knew and loved, longing to rest beside them again? It is a chilling thought!

A third theory is connected to section 34 of the cemetery. This area is known as the Soldiers' Lot and contains the graves of those lost in the Civil War, the Spanish-American War, and World War I. Though this part of the cemetery is believed to be extremely haunted, the graves of those who died during the Civil War are said to have the *most* paranormal activity. You already know that many claim to have seen the apparitions of the soldiers who died in the camp near the football stadium. The prisoners' spirits have been spotted at Forest Hill Cemetery as well.

There are 240 Union soldiers and 140 Confederate soldiers buried in the cemetery. The ghostly figures of Confederate soldiers are seen most often, but people have also seen the spirits of Union soldiers roaming through the gravesites. Could it be that because these men were bitter enemies in life, their spirits find it difficult to rest in peace so close to one another? Are they still fighting a war that ended more than 150 years ago . . . from *beyond the grave*?

Then again, it's possible the Union soldiers are restless in death for another reason. After all, it is not just soldiers who are buried in section 34.

Also buried here are the bodies of eight children who died while in the care of the

Soldiers' Orphan Home. The home cared for the children of Union soldiers orphaned during the war. Buried together, the children did not receive a grave marker until 1873. Perhaps the spirits of Union men killed in battle roam the grounds looking for children they left behind? It is a heartbreaking theory.

Ghostly sightings of soldiers are a frequent occurrence inside the gates of Forest Hill. Those who have a sensitivity to paranormal experiences notice eerie feelings as they walk through the cemetery.

Some report becoming overwhelmed by emotion while walking the grounds. These people describe deep sorrow and dread when exploring the property. Others experience physical sensations, like headaches and stomachaches, in the area where the soldiers are buried.

We may never know why the spirits of Forest Hill Cemetery are so restless. (At least, not until we join them on the other side.) All we can be sure of is that whatever keeps these ghosts connected to the land seems to have a tight hold on them... and it shows no sign of letting up!

The Ghost of Seminole Highway

Legend has it that a ghost on Seminole Highway is as old as Madison itself. Maybe even older. Years ago, the part of the highway that now runs along the west side of the Arboretum wound around settler Daniel Damon Bryant's farm. Back then, the road was known as Bryant Road. Madisonians had another name for it: *Ghost Road.*

In the time before streetlights and sidewalks, when people traveled the rural road at night, they carried lanterns or walked by moonlight.

It was on those dark, lonely stretches of road that countless late-night travelers claim to have encountered a ghost. The specter would appear as a softly glowing white mist. Often, the spirit would emerge from the brush that lined both sides of the road.

Terrified travelers would walk down the middle of the road, trying to steer clear of the ghostly form. But that wasn't enough to avoid the otherworldly being that haunted old highway.

Those who encountered the misty figure claimed its

shimmering form would follow them down the dark, deserted road. Once the spirit appeared, it might trail the living for a few yards—or a few miles. Then, without warning, the ghost would disappear just as suddenly as it arrived.

The ghost never spoke to or attempted to harm the frightened walkers, but there was no way to predict what it might suddenly do. All who traveled the lonely road after dark feared the spirit. For years, people avoided the road at night whenever possible.

However, the shimmering specter wasn't the only creature known to haunt the area. Nearby farmers and property owners claimed that they also encountered a *ghostly pony* on the haunted roadway.

They reported hearing the "pounding hoof beats of an unshod pony" trotting up and down the road at night. But in the morning, there was never any trace that the animal had been there—not even a single hoofprint.

Despite the many claims of paranormal encounters along the haunted road, no one was ever able to determine who—or *what*—the restless spirit was. Or why, exactly, the spirit continued to linger among the living.

At the time, locals enjoyed gathering around campfires late at night to tell the stories of those who'd encountered the unexplained on Ghost Road. Sometimes, they would speculate that the spirit was that of a young Indigenous boy who had yet to crossover to the other side. Others believed the spirit was that of a murdered man buried in a nearby cemetery. No one knew for certain, but that didn't stop people from sharing spooky tales long after most sensible people had gone to bed.

These stories thrilled and terrified generations of Madisonians but never led to any answers. As the area became more populated, sightings of the shimmering spirit became rarer but did not disappear entirely.

Sometime in the late 1930s, when cars replaced theo nce-common horse-drawn buggies, Bryant Road was renamed Seminole Highway.

Some say all the changes to the area chased the spirit of Ghost Road away, while others believe the spirit never left. Is the ghost that reportedly haunts Seminole Highway nothing more than a legend from long ago? Or could the spirit still be out there, its shimmering mist sparkling in the moonlight?

These days, it might be hard to catch a glimpse of the ghostly form, with all the traffic and streetlights that line the once lonely roadway. But that doesn't mean you should stop looking for it. If you happen to be traveling

down Seminole Highway late at night, keep your eyes on the shoulder of the road.

You never know what might appear just outside your car window. On second thought, maybe you'll *want* to keep your eyes tightly shut as you drive down the dark road...

The choice is yours. Choose wisely, or you may live to regret it.

Mysterious Waterways

There are 15,074 lakes in Wisconsin. Madison is surrounded by five of them: Lake Mendota, Lake Monona, Lake Waubesa, Lake Wingra, and Lake Kegonsa. These lakes are all connected by the sixty-two-mile-long Yahara River. That's a lot of water!

But it's what's *lurking* in all of that water that is more interesting. For generations, there have been countless eyewitness accounts of a mysterious monster swimming through Madison's chain of lakes.

Reports of this strange creature have come from all five lakes. The monster is sometimes described as having a long, spiked tail. Others have noted its large jaws and blazing eyes. The beast has been blamed for overturning canoes with its tail, chasing sailboats, and destroying piers.

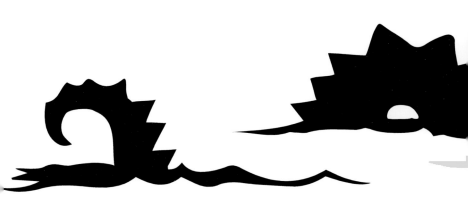

Some are certain the animal is an unknown sea serpent. But others believe it is Winnebozho. In the Ojibwe culture, Winnebozho is thought to be the creator of plant and animal life. It is a real creature and has always lived in the lakes.

What do you think? Could there *really* be a monster lurking beneath the waves of Madison's lakes? Let's dive in and find out! We'll start with Lake Mendota, the first and largest lake in the Yahara Chain.

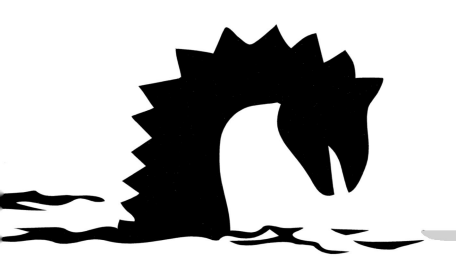

We'll have to go all the way back to 1860 to find the first documented sighting of this mysterious water monster. On a beautiful day, a couple decided to take a canoe out on the lake and head to Governor's Island. The sun was shining and their paddles cut through the water with ease as they made their way across the lake. When they got close to the island, one of their paddles hit something just beneath the surface of the water.

At first, the pair though they hit a submerged log—at least until the log thrashed

around and then dove underwater! The couple was stunned. What animal was so large and solid that it could be mistaken for a log? They were too frightened to stick around and find out. The couple quickly paddled toward land as fast as they could.

But the more they thought about what had happened, the less it seemed to make sense. Sure, there are fish in the lake, lots of them. But bass and walleye aren't anywhere *near* as large as a log. Even a massive muskie isn't as

big around as a log. What in the world had they encountered on their canoe trip?

The couple started to share their story with friends and family in Madison. Soon after, people began to whisper that an unknown creature was lurking beneath the waters of Lake Mendota.

Then, in the summer of 1883, the mysterious creature reappeared and made headlines in Madison newspapers.

A local fisherman, Billy Dunn, and his wife were fishing on the lake at eleven in the morning, when the pair spotted something strange in the water. Squinting in the sunlight, Billy saw something black in the lake. When

he took a closer look, he noticed that it was *moving*. Right toward him and his boat!

As he watched the black object slide through the water, Billy thought it looked like a snake. The animal slithered closer to the boat. Then suddenly, it began to rise from the lake! What came to the surface was a creature Billy had never seen before.

Billy was shocked when something that he described as having a "reptile head" arose from the water. The creature was about two feet above the waves. Though it had looked black from the boat, Billy and his wife then saw it had light-colored skin with white spots—and it was definitely slimy. When the snake-like

animal finally reached their boat, it flicked its long, black, forked tongue at them. Billy's eyes went wide when the creature opened its mouth and revealed sharp, black fangs!

Terrified, Billy struck the monster on the back of its neck with his boat oar. He was afraid the beast was going to bite them. Or maybe something even worse! The blow stunned the monster, but only for a moment. To Billy's horror, the creature quickly recovered and sank its dark fangs into the wooden oar!

Billy began to hit the monster and did not stop until it released his oar. After Billy wrestled the oar away from the creature, it disappeared beneath the surface of the water.

The shaken man and wife took a moment to calm down. They could not believe what had just happened. It was an incredible story, but they felt pretty sure people would believe them. After all, Billy had some amazing proof of his encounter with the mysterious beast. Embedded in his oar were the creature's long, black fangs!

Once they were safely back on shore, Billy told the story of his encounter with the beast far and wide. If anyone didn't quite believe his tall tale, Billy would simply show them the oar with the black fangs still stuck deep inside the wood. Eventually, Billy sold that oar to a Chicago musician. While the evidence was

no longer in Madison, the stories of the lake creature continued.

In 1917, a famous Wisconsin historian named Charles Brown recorded a story he'd heard about a strange discovery on the shore at Picnic Point, a slip of land across from Governor's Island. Picnic Point is a peninsula along the southern shores of Lake Mendota. It is one of the most visited spots inside the university's Lakeshore Nature Preserve.

As the story goes, university students were strolling along the shoreline when they found something on the beach they could not identify. To them, it looked like a fish scale, but it was larger than any scale they had ever seen. They decided to take the massive scale and show it to a professor on campus. Legend has it that the professor identified the object as a scale ... from a sea serpent!

Hard to believe, right? Well, soon after the

scale was identified, a man finishing at Picnic Point reported a terrifying encounter with a bizarre creature that came to the surface of the lake.

The man said the thing he saw had a snake-like head, "large jaws," and "blazing eyes." When he'd first caught sight of the beast, the man froze in fear. He watched in terror as the animal slithered through the water. When he could finally move again, the fisherman ran as fast as he could away from whatever that thing was. He was so frightened, he left his fishing rod and all his gear behind.

That same year, a pair of sunbathing college students had their own surprising encounter with the lake beast. The young man and woman had laid out their beach towels on a dock. As they lay there soaking up the sunshine, the young woman felt something tickle the soles of her feet. She rolled over on her towel to scold her friend to stop tickling her.

But when the young woman opened her eyes, the words got stuck in her throat. Right in front of her was something she'd never forget! Instead of her friend, she saw a hideous creature with what looked like the head of a snake or a dragon. The creature's forked black

tongue flickered across the soles of her feet! She let out an ear-piercing shriek!

Startled, the young man sat up to see what the commotion was about. He could not believe his eyes when he saw the creature and its terrible flickering tongue! The students had seen enough! They jumped up from their beach towels and ran to the safety of a nearby fraternity house. In the end, the woman's feet were fine, but her nerves, not so much.

Pretty strange stuff, right? If you think you can avoid whatever lurks beneath the water by staying away from Lake Mendota, I have bad news for you. Strange creatures have been spotted in Lake Monona as well! Read on to find out what is hiding on the other side of the isthmus.

In 1892, a fisherman from a village just south of Madison had a terrifying encounter with an unusual beast while on Lake Monona. The day started off an ordinary one. The fisherman rented a boat and rowed it out to what he thought would be an ideal fishing spot.

While he was putting bait on his fishing hook, however, he noticed ripples in the murky water. As he peered over the edge of his boat, he spotted a bizarre creature with a flat head rising from the depths of the lake. Before the man had the chance to flee, the creature's head splashed to the surface, right next to his boat!

The man was staring into the face of a snaky beast that he believed to be at least twenty feet long! The creature lunged toward the man and then dove under the rowboat. The frightened man was sure the creature was trying to overturn his boat! He decided not to stick around to find out what would happen next. He dropped his fishing pole into the lake, grabbed both oars, and rowed furiously to the shore. From that day on, the fisherman was done with Lake Monona. Once he was back on dry land, he vowed to never go out on the lake again.

But the fisherman's experience did not stop people from boating on the lake. Instead, droves of people arrived, eager to catch a glimpse of the beast for themselves. And guess what? Later that same summer, there was *another* strange encounter with an unknown creature in the water.

It was a warm, sunny day when two teenage boys decided to paddle a canoe from Hoboken

Beach to a beach near Winnequah Park. They stayed close to the shore as they traveled north on the lake. One of the boys stopped paddling when he suddenly spotted something in the water about seventy-five feet from their canoe. Whatever was in the water was moving quickly—and coming right for them!

The other boy soon saw the creature as well. He caught a glimpse of what appeared to be its head and thought it might be a dogfish. Then, to his shock, the creature rose from the waves! Instead of swimming below the water's surface, like other fish in Lake Monona, it moved just like a dolphin, diving in and out of the water as it headed toward the boys' canoe. The boys in

the canoe were mystified. But they weren't the only ones. People on the nearby beach saw the beast as well.

Suddenly, panicked screams filled the air. Swimmers raced out of the water to the safety of the shore. People on land reported that the creature appeared ten to fifteen feet long, with a circumference of around one foot.

After terrifying everyone in sight, the beast simply swam away. No one was harmed, but everyone was frightened. They wondered what they had just seen. And ... when it might return.

It took some time, but five years later, the creature was back. It was a warm June day in

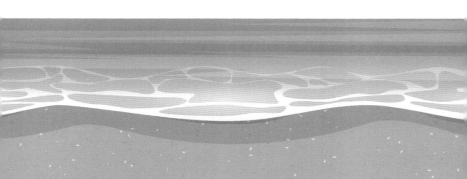

1897 when a man named Eugene Heath spotted the much-talked-about creature from shore. Eugene decided that enough was enough. He was tired of people being afraid of a "monster" in Monona. Whatever the creature was, it needed to be removed from the lake, and he would be the one to do it.

Eugene picked up his gun. He raised the weapon and aimed at the creature swimming in the water. Then, he pulled the trigger. The sound of gunfire got the attention of others on the shore, and some of them could see what Eugene was shooting at.

Eugene fired a second shot, but instead of swimming away from the gunfire, the creature swam toward it! Heart racing, Eugene fired his

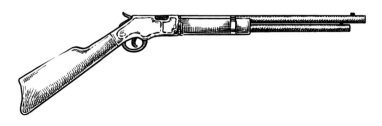

gun again and again before the animal finally turned and swam away from shore. Eugene and the crowd on the beach watched the creature, enthralled as they were frightened, until it vanished beneath the waves.

Most who witnessed the astonishing event did not think Eugene's bullets had hit the animal. And even if they *had*, people seemed pretty certain the creature had not been seriously injured. Those people were probably right. Because later that night, eyewitnesses around Lake Monona claimed to spot the creature gliding once again along the moonlit lake.

The creature in Lake Monona has not been spotted for a long time. Maybe it really has disappeared? Or... maybe it's just gotten better at hiding. Some people believe the beast is simply spending more time in the other lakes in the chain. After all, it wasn't very long after those university students discovered the strange scales on Picnic Point that something eerie was spotted in Lake Waubesa.

One summer day, a vacationing fisherman from Illinois rowed his boat onto Lake Waubesa. Once he had found a fishing spot he liked, he anchored his boat and cast his fishing line into the water. Within moments, the water around his boat started churning. For a second, it seemed like he had picked the perfect place to fish! But suddenly, a great beast rose to the surface. The fisherman could not believe what he was seeing!

A dark green creature that looked to be between sixty and seventy feet long emerged from the lake's depths right in front of him. The animal appeared to be sunning itself on the surface of the water and did not seem to have noticed the man or his boat. The fisherman wanted it to stay that way.

Very quietly, the man raised his anchor. The great beast did not stir. Now, he had to row away without disturbing the creature. He eased his oars into the water with barely a ripple. The creature remained motionless. Gently, he pulled the oars through the water, careful to avoid any splashing. He kept moving forward, silently gliding through the water. He kept as quiet as possible until he could no longer see the beast.

Once he was safely on land, the man ran to tell people what he had seen in the lake. But no one believed him. That is, until a few weeks later.

Not long after the fisherman's eerie encounter

on the lake, a couple was swimming near Waubesa Beach. The pair swam side by side, every kick of their legs and stroke of their arms pulling them farther and farther from the shore.

Once they were a good distance from the beach, a strange beast rose suddenly from the water. It was close enough that the swimmers could see the creature's eyes glittering in the sun. The beast did not move, but it stared directly at the pair, sending a chill through their bones. Terrified, they turned away from the creature and swam for safety as fast as they could. They did not stop for a single moment, not even to look behind them to see if the creature was following them back to shore.

The couple reached the beach, out of breath and exhausted, but safe. Had they just encountered the same creature that the fisherman from Illinois had seen? Some people were certain they had!

As you may have already guessed, the creature did not stop there. Several people claimed to have seen a dragon-like animal in the water near Colladay Bay and Williams Point, and it has also been spotted in Lake Kegonsa. (Yes, even smaller lakes and bays have not been immune to sightings!)

Lake Wingra had a scare of its own, with people claiming to have seen a lake monster lurking in its waters, but it later turned out that it was not a monster after all. (Instead, when

people went to investigate what they'd seen, it turned out to be a very large snapping turtle caught in fishing equipment.) But that doesn't mean the beast—if such a creature truly does exist—hasn't visited Lake Wingra. Though sightings of the mysterious lake monster have decreased considerably since the late 1800s, it may just be doing a good job of hiding itself.

After all, just because you can't see something...*doesn't* mean it isn't there. So the next time you are in a boat on Madison's chain of lakes or sailing down the Yahara River, stay alert! Whether you believe it or not, strange things are known to lurk beneath the surface of these waters.

CHAPTER 7

The Beast of Bray Road

Have you ever wondered if werewolves exist? In Wisconsin, the answer depends on who you ask. If you ask that question in Elkhorn, a city about sixty miles southeast of Madison, the response is likely to send a shiver down your spine.

Something prowling in the shadows has terrified residents of Elkhorn for decades. People call it The Beast of Bray Road, but only because no one knows exactly what the creature is. People who have seen the frightening creature can't agree about its appearance. One thing eye witnesses *can* agree on, however, is that the chilling creature is neither human nor any known animal—and that the Beast of Bray Road is the most fearsome thing they've ever seen!

Bray Road is a single-lane, rural road in Walworth County. There are no streetlights nor sidewalks along the lonely road. The pavement cuts through farm fields and forests believed to be the home of the dreaded beast.

The first time someone reported seeing the snarling creature was back in 1936. Just after midnight, a security guard at a residential care facility was patrolling the grounds. The building was nestled in the woods, far outside the city limits. The guard sometimes spotted raccoons trying to get into the trash or families of opossums foraging for food, but that was it. Walking the grounds with his flashlight, he expected another quiet night.

But as the security guard made his rounds, the beam of his flashlight suddenly shone on a wild creature clawing at the ground. The guard approached the beast cautiously. He got the shock of his life when, suddenly, the creature rose from its haunches. The guard could not believe his eyes! Standing on its hind legs, the creature was over six feet tall! The beast was covered in dark hair and reeked of rotting flesh.

The creature slowly turned its head toward the guard. It stared into the man's eyes and growled. It was a deep growl that sounded nothing like that of a dog, or any other animal, for that matter. To the guard, the sound was otherworldly.

The creature continued to stare at the terrified guard. As he slowly crept away, the guard could feel the beast's eyes on him. The beast did not harm the guard, but he left the man filled with fear. The guard never encountered the creature again, but others in Walworth County would not be as lucky.

Sightings of the mysterious creature continue to this day. So many people have reported seeing the creature prowling around the Bray Road area, they named the creature after the rural road itself. For many years, the beast was thought to be a local legend. Then a writer named Linda Godfrey interviewed some of the people who reported seeing the beast in the 1980s and 1990s. She hoped her work would help reveal the identity of the creature that had frightened so many people in the area.

The eyewitnesses Linda spoke with for her research had many different descriptions of the creature they had seen. Many of them said the creature stood on two legs. Some people thought the beast was around five feet tall. Others said it was seven feet tall! Some described the creature as having a shaggy coat of long dark hair. But there have also been reports that the beast was covered in fur that had streaks of silver or white.

Most people described the creature's head as similar to that of a German Shepherd. They said the beast had an elongated muzzle and pointed ears, just like the popular dog breed. However, more than a few eyewitnesses said the beast's head looked more like an ape than a dog.

Some people claimed that the thing moved like a human, while others said it moved just like a panther. Some believed the creature was not of this world. They thought that a being so frightening must have been conjured from the underworld.

But all who'd spotted the beast mentioned one similar detail—its terrifying eyes! Each described the same intense, penetrating stare from the creature's cold, yellow eyes. Every eyewitness shivered with horror when describing those terrible eyes.

Linda Godfrey never discovered what the beast was, but she did make the beast famous. People could not get enough of the stories Linda wrote about encounters with

the creature. Before long, newspapers and TV shows across the United States were reporting on the beast. The idea that a possible werewolf lived in Elkhorn, Wisconsin, turned out to be big news! Before long, curious people came from all over the country to drive along Bray Road at night in hopes of spotting the creature.

Throughout the years, many people have tried to uncover the identity of the mysterious creature. A lot of people have dismissed the notion that the creature is something mythical like a werewolf. But despite their best efforts, no one has been able to prove the mystery

beast is a wolf, bear, stray dog, or some other animal.

What do you think? Does a werewolf live in Elkhorn? As unbelievable as it sounds, that just might be the case! But what will it take to discover the identity of the Beast of Bray Road? And who would be daring enough to take on the job? Perhaps *you* . . . ?

A Ghostly Goodbye

Thanks for exploring the spooky side of Madison with us!

It seems like just about anywhere you go in Madison, you might run into a ghost or some strange, unexplained creature! There are some seriously scary things in the city. After reading these tales, you might want to hide under the covers and skip visiting the sights around Madison to avoid all strange and otherworldly encounters. And honestly, we can't blame you. Or maybe you are inspired to do your own paranormal investigations. Yikes!

If you *do* decide to go exploring in hopes of having your own ghostly encounter, watch out! You just might get more than you bargained for. After all, ghosts that seem a little spooky in the book might be TERRIFYING in real life!

If you decide to seek out the spirits for yourself, it's important to follow a few basic rules. Stick to places you are allowed to enter. Many people do not welcome ghost hunters on their property. If you get permission to seek out the spirits, make sure your ghostly

adventure is a safe one. Remember to stay in a group, take notes, and always—and I mean ALWAYS!—watch your back.

In Madison, Wisconsin, you never know who, or *what*, might be right behind you!

Anna Lardinois tingles the spines of Milwaukee locals and visitors through her haunted, historical walking tours known as Gothic Milwaukee. The former English teacher is an ardent collector of stories, an avid walker, and a sweet treat enthusiast. She happily resides in a historic home in Milwaukee that, at this time, does not appear to be haunted. Visit her at www.annalardinois.com to find out more!

Check out some of the other *Spooky America* titles available now!

Spooky America was adapted from the creeptastic *Haunted America* series for adults. *Haunted America* explores historical haunts in cities and regions across America. Here's more from the original *Madison Ghosts and Legends* author, Anna Lardinois:

www.annalardinois.com